D1539817

LEADERSHIP SKILLS

LEADERSHIP SKILLS
by Diane E. Rossiter

THE CAREER SKILLS LIBRARY

Communication Skills
By Richard Worth

Information Management
By Joseph Mackall

Leadership Skills
By Diane E. Rossiter

Learning the Ropes
By Sharon Naylor

Organization Skills
By Richard Worth

Problem-Solving
By Dandi Daley Mackall

Self-Development
By Dandi Daley Mackall

Teamwork Skills
By Dandi Daley Mackall

A New England Publishing Associates Book

Printed in the United States of America
U-8

Library of Congress Cataloging-in-Publication Data

Rossiter, Diane E.
    Leadership skills / by Diane E. Rossiter.
        p.   cm. — (The career skills library)
    Includes bibliographical references and index.
    ISBN 0-89434-213-4
    1. Leadership. 2. Management. 3. Teams in the workplace. I. Title II. Series
    HD57.7R686   1998
    658.4'092—dc21   97-26453
                                    CIP

CONTENTS

INTRODUCTION

When we think of leaders, we think of people like Abraham Lincoln, Martin Luther King Jr. or Mahatma Gandhi. But all of us have the potential to be leaders—at school, in our communities, and at work.

Many people have no desire to be leaders; they are content to be contributors. However, in much of today's world, teamwork is necessary to get things done. And teams without leaders usually are ineffective in achieving their goals. They flounder without a leader's help to focus on the goal and to make choices that will move the team toward that goal.

In school and extracurricular activities, you may be able to avoid the responsibilities of leadership. Someone else usually will step forward. But in the workplace, the choice will not always be yours. When you are assigned a project, you will most likely need to rely on the help and support of others. These people, in effect, become your team. To get the most out of their efforts, you will need to exercise good leadership.

A leader inspires others to act by setting a good example. His drive and perseverence spurs others on.

(V. Harlow/Vinal Regional Vocational Technical School, Middletown, CT)

A team leader offers guidance to other members of his group so they can finish the project on time. A leader's motivation inspires others to use their abilities in order to reach a common goal.

A leader's job is to help others make their best contribution toward a shared goal.

He strives to be the best *he* can be—not to outcompete others. In fact, a leader's job is to help others make their best contribution toward a shared goal.

A leader motivates others through mutual trust. She trusts in their ability and willingness to pursue the goal; they trust in her ability and willingness to give them the support they need. This mutual trust is essential in building a team that will be successful in reaching its goal.

10

In today's workplace, you will need to develop leadership skills to build and direct teams to get work done. Although some leadership qualities are inborn, many of the skills necessary for good leadership can be learned. In this book, we'll discuss ways of interacting with others that will help you lead them to success. Topics include:

- ▶ Motivating others
- ▶ Giving and taking criticism
- ▶ Organizing a project
- ▶ Delegating responsibility
- ▶ Monitoring the team's progress
- ▶ Learning leadership skills on the job

CHAPTER ONE
LEADERSHIP—
WHAT IT IS AND
WHY IT MATTERS

"Peter, I need you to prepare a report on our company's services for a prospective new client," said his boss. "We've been trying to get their business for more than a year. You've got decent computer graphic skills. Make the report look good."

Although Peter only started working four months ago, he hopes to become an assistant manager as soon as a vacancy occurs. "Thank goodness for that computer design course I took last summer. Doing a good job on this report might help me get the promotion I deserve," he thought.

Peter has been frustrated that his efforts at work up to this point have not been recognized by his supervisor. Peter always gets to work early, stays late, and often works through lunch. He's proud that he usually is able to finish his assignments well before they are due. He looks down on his coworkers who seem content to take all the allotted time to complete their work.

It doesn't bother him that none of his coworkers even says hello anymore, but he deeply cares that no one in management seems to know how good his work is. This new client report may finally get their attention.

He knows he will need help from other staff members to complete the report. Fortunately, he can make them put aside their individual projects to supply him with what he needs to do his report. When one clerk seems deliberately slow in finding a file he needs, a reminder that "The Boss" has put *him* in charge is all it takes.

Peter also keeps after the department secretary to type up each part of the report as soon as he produces it. Since he prides himself on finishing every project early, he tells the staff that the report is due in three days, instead of the actual deadline the following week. "I'm the only one who cares," he thinks, as his coworkers grumble about working late two nights in a row.

Peter is glad that his boss finally seems to be aware of how hard he works. He smiles to himself when he notices his boss watching him more and more. Since Peter is a perfectionist, he would naturally check and recheck every detail anyway; having his boss see him in action is just a well-deserved bonus.

When the report is finished, Peter knows that he has done an excellent job. "This will really do it," he thinks. Later his boss says the report is a "thorough, competent effort." Peter is disappointed. He had expected higher praise. He also is disappointed a few weeks later with his six-month review. His supervisor had not given him very good ratings in the categories "leadership" and "potential for promotion."

"I stand on my head and it's not enough," he thinks. "I'm smarter than most of the managers, and I work harder. What's it going to take to convince them?"

WHAT CHARACTERISTICS MAKE A LEADER?

Leaders must certainly be able to do the job, but ability alone is not enough. True leadership requires a willingness to be bold, to consider unusual approaches to problems, to not just follow the tried-and-true. Leaders are self-confident and have no need to put others down to feel good about themselves. They *are* willing to stand up for their ideas and debate them with others. This kind of intellectual competition is characteristic of a good leader. In *Planning for Nonplanners*, Darryl Ellis and Peter Pekar Jr. call this being "constructively competitive." They also note

(Joe Duffy)

"He may seem a little TOO 'Gung-Ho!' at first...but he does know how to motivate the others."

Exceptional leaders know how to be competitive without alienating others.

that exceptional leaders know how to be competitive without alienating others.

This may be difficult for young employees who think the way to get ahead is to outshine their co-workers. But neither workers nor supervisors like or respect someone who thinks only of himself. The staff of Catalyst, a national nonprofit organization devoted to career advancement for women, suggests keeping a low profile while new on the job. In *Making the Most of Your First Job,* the Catalyst staff notes that if you're too "gung ho," especially at first, people will resent you. Resentful coworkers certainly will not be motivated to cooperate with you.

GETTING ALONG WITH OTHERS

Above all, leadership requires the ability to get along with others in a variety of situations. A class president won't be able to accomplish much if she begins to think too highly of herself. Classmates she snubs are not likely to volunteer to help with the prom decorations. Likewise, an assistant manager who ignores his coworkers until he needs something will not always get the results he wants.

In *Why Employees Don't Do What They're Supposed to Do and What to Do About It,* Ferdinand F. Fournies reminds managers to treat their staff members with such common courtesies as saying "please" and "thank you," apologizing for being late to a meeting and not interrupting people while they are speaking. Other leaders in business and industry recommend the old-fashioned Golden Rule: Treat others as you would like to be treated.

The workplace is still primarily a place where people interact. The social skills we have been practicing all our lives are important in business, too. Fournies tells managers to look at people's faces when they are talking, to avoid sarcastic comments, and to control emotional outbursts. Sarcasm and temper tantrums are not acceptable in a social setting, and even less so in the workplace. Being in a supervisory position doesn't give you the right to be discourteous.

A GOOD LEADER IS SENSITIVE

Although very important, courtesy and agreeableness are not enough for good leadership. A leader also must be sensitive to the feelings and needs of others. These needs are not always clearly expressed. Sometimes people do not even know what they want or need. A talented leader is able to "read" the people around him and to adjust his own behavior.

Alissa, college student and part-time office manager for a local nonprofit organization, says the hardest part of her job is figuring out her coworkers. "When Ellie drags her feet on an assignment, it probably means she doesn't feel capable of doing it. Maybe I'll need to give her some more help. When Jerry 'forgets' I asked him to do something, it might mean I've been pushing him too hard—I do rely on him a lot because we're such a small staff."

Alissa already has learned to pick up on her coworkers' cues and act accordingly. Her sensitivity and support motivate her staff and make her an effective leader.

EXERCISE

Earlier in this chapter, we learned about how insensitive Peter was to his coworkers and his supervisor. Reread the story and find three cues he missed. Tell how he could have changed his behavior in response to those cues.

ABILITY AND HARD WORK ARE NOT ENOUGH

Paul is a junior in high school. He already knows he wants to major in math when he goes to college. Paul has gone to information sessions at several colleges, and he has begun to worry. The admissions officers always stress that good grades are not enough. Colleges are interested in what a student can do outside of the classroom, too. The more selective colleges look for students who have also shown leadership ability in their extracurricular activities.

Paul has been a member of the high school Key Club, a service organization, for three years. He decided to ask his friend Scott, the current president, to nominate him to be next year's president. "I think I deserve it," Paul thought. "I never miss a meeting and I'm willing to do anything they ask me. I've helped at every car wash, distributed turkeys at Thanksgiving and even volunteered at the Senior Citizen Center every Tuesday. And I know I'd be better than anybody else at keeping track of the money we raise for charity."

FACTOID:

Leaders need to work through others to be successful. About 50% to 60% of leaders fail because they are unable to build and guide an effective team.

Paul certainly has contributed much to the Key Club. He always has been a conscientious and capable worker. But Scott was hesitant to promise to nominate Paul. He decided to speak to the club advisor about his worries.

This has been a harder job than I thought it would be. Running the meetings and keeping everybody interested in our long-term projects were the hardest, I guess. And the Key Club is a really large bunch. I think some of the kids are only in it for the social scene.

Others mean well, but they say they'll do something and then they don't. Sometimes I felt like being a drill-sergeant type, but I knew that wouldn't work. I had to figure out ways to make them take responsibility without being a heavy. I don't think Paul has it in him. He's not a "people person."

The advisor agreed. She and Scott decided to ask Paul if he would be interested in running for the office of club treasurer. Although Paul was disappointed, he secretly also was relieved. "I don't know why I thought I'd like to be in charge. I'm not good with people, like Scott. Maybe I'd just better stick to what I'm good at," he thought.

A DEGREE IS NO GUARANTEE

People often think they are good at something because they have done well in a school setting. But a good grade, a diploma, or even a college degree is no guarantee of success in the workplace. In fact, the brilliant student is often *too* smart for his own good. He thinks no one can tell him anything, and so he cannot learn.

With surprising frequency, individuals who were academic superstars in high school, college, and even business school, have dramatically less success in their managerial careers.

**—Richard K. Wagner
and Robert J. Sternberg,**
Measures of Leadership

Robert Sternberg and Richard Wagner's research revealed that academic leaders often "flop" when they switch to the workplace. The reason? They lack the practical knowledge and "street smarts" it takes to be a "star" at work. This doesn't mean they will never get ahead. They may just have to give it some time, "learn the ropes."

The staff of Catalyst, in *Making the Most of Your First Job,* gives this advice:

You've got to learn what's going on before you deliver your opinion on it. Some people become overanxious when they start a job— they become pushy. If you lay low at first, when you do open your mouth everyone will really listen and you'll have the advantage of being much better informed. In an office environment, everyday experience rates higher

On-the-job experience is valuable knowledge that is not earned by attending school. If you're at work and need help, or just a reliable opinion, ask someone who's been on the job longer than you. Even if that person works under *you, he or she probably will be more familiar with how things run.*

than a genius IQ. Unlike a mathematical equation, office problems aren't always clear-cut. Perhaps you don't have all the information you need to understand, let alone solve, the problem. Or perhaps there will be several solutions to your problem, each with its own plusses and minuses. Only practical, on-the-job experience can help you accurately weigh your options and make the best choice for your company.

People who have been on the job longer than you can be a great help. Asking others for their opinions will not make you seem less capable. In fact, it indicates a willingness to learn. And it does not matter if the experienced worker is lower than you in the company. It is their *experience* that counts.

Asking others for their opinions will not make you seem less capable.

Another kind of knowledge that you can only pick up on the job is the company's unwritten rules. One executive in the Wagner and Sternberg study describes this as knowing "what goes without saying around here." New employees need to keep their eyes and ears open and, generally, their mouths shut. Having too much to say too soon is a sure path to saying *exactly* the wrong thing. Then you lose the respect of your coworkers.

EXERCISE

Describe a time you were the "new kid on the block." Was there something you did or said that you now realize was a mistake? What could you have done differently?

LEADERSHIP STYLE

When Richard was chosen to direct a long-term project at the firm where he worked, his coworkers were delighted. Richard's projects usually went well and everybody always ended up feeling good about his or her work.

While his bosses valued Richard's initiative and creative thinking, his staff more often praised his flexibility and openness to suggestions. These qualities make his staff feel they have something to contribute. In fact, Richard's attitude encourages *them* to be creative, and to take initiative, too.

"At meetings, I feel safe speaking my mind," said one coworker.

"We don't always have to do everything his way," said another.

"I'm interested in what my staff thinks," says Richard. "Their input is important to me. I'm not a very 'top down' kind of guy. Good ideas can come from anywhere."

Some leaders are comfortable with employee participation in problem solving. Like Richard, they feel there is a lot to be gained. Others manage employees with a more directive style. Sometimes the style will depend on the type of project or on the individuals included in the work team. A "top-down" style might be best for a complicated project with many parts or for a team whose members are mostly new, entry-level employees. But usually a leader's style is just that—his style.

Having a leadership style makes things easier for your employees. They come to know what to expect. If you usually welcome their ideas, they won't expect you to suddenly jump on a staff member who has a suggestion. On the other hand, if you usually give a lot of exact instructions for performing an assignment, your staff has probably come to depend on that. They will be uncomfortable if you tell them to "do whatever you think is best." A consistent approach helps build trust.

A consistent approach helps build trust.

TRUST

People respond to leaders they can trust. They need to be able to count on their leader to do the right thing, whether it's in school, a club, or a job.

When a teacher changes the assignment without giving enough notice, students can't do a good job. On top of that, the students now do not feel as much trust for their teacher.

When you agree to be in charge of a committee, others are depending on you.

They are willing to be workers, but you have accepted the responsibility of leading them. Don't let them down, or you will lose their trust.

Raymond was in charge of the advertisers' program for the sports banquet. The members of his committee were to visit local businesses to ask them to support school sports by buying an ad in the program. Raymond had lots of volunteers for his committee because the money from the ads would benefit all the school's teams. Also, Raymond had promised the volunteers that he would provide them with lists of local stores that participated in the past.

Gary, last year's chairperson, had given Raymond a folder to help get him started. It included copies of the programs for the last several years. Gary also had made notes about the best times to visit particular businesses and with whom to speak. When Raymond had mentioned this at the sports council meeting, it really hooked a lot of volunteers.

"I usually hate soliciting donations and things," said Sandy. "But it makes a difference if you know who to ask for, and that they've done it before."

Unfortunately, Raymond had misplaced the folder. "I'm sure it will turn up soon," he told himself. "I'll bring it in soon," he told everybody else. "I'm retyping it."

After looking at home and in his locker, Raymond began to think he had accidentally thrown the folder out. His mother suggested he ask Gary's mother for his phone number at college. Maybe Gary had kept all the information on his computer.

"If I tell Gary I lost the folder, he'll think I'm a dope," Raymond thought to himself. "If I tell the volunteers I don't have the information I promised, some of them might drop out. I'd better not say anything to anybody until the kick-off meeting. They wouldn't walk out on the meeting. We'll just have to use the phone book. I know some of the kids will be upset, but they'll just have to deal with it."

At the kick-off meeting a few days later, he asked Sandy to go to the office to get a phone book. When Sandy realized that it was for making lists of businesses from the yellow pages, she felt cheated.

"I should never have volunteered," she thought. "And I never *would* have if I had known it would be like this."

Sandy was probably not the only one who felt that way. An unexpected change in our situation makes us uncomfortable. Some people are able to rise to the challenge of the new circumstances. Others may not be able to. But in either case, like Sandy, they will feel cheated.

THE TRUST BUSTERS

1. *The Blabber* tells people everyone else's business. A person in a leadership position sometimes has access to private information. This does not give them the privilege of telling anyone else.

2. *The Manipulator* may only tell you what she wants you to know. She uses deception, or plays on people's fears or emotions to get what she wants. This is controlling, not leading.

3. *The Exploiter* takes advantage of others. His position may give him power, but misusing it will cause resentment and resistance.

4. *The Stealer* always takes more than her share. She takes more privileges for herself. She takes the best assignments. And she takes the credit for others' work and ideas.

5. *The Agree-er* is much more pleasant to be around. She always is ready to give others a pat on the back. The problem is, others don't really know where they stand with her. A good leader is also a teacher who helps others improve by giving them his or her honest reaction.

6. *The Avoider* is also dishonest in his reactions. He will say, "I'll think about it," because he doesn't want to say, "No." He deals with unpleasant situations by simply avoiding them. This puts more pressure and responsibility on others.

F A C T O I D :

In several studies done between 1988 and 1992, workers rated trustworthiness as the most important element of leadership.

No one feels comfortable with a supervisor who tells Employee A one thing and Employee B another or a coworker who says one thing and does another. Why would anyone do this? The answer is usually office politics. Some people say or do whatever they think will help them get ahead. Dealing with these kinds of people is very difficult. We soon lose our trust and respect for them.

There are other ways people can lose our trust. You may recognize a friend, or even yourself, in some of the categories in the box on "The Trust Busters." But a leader who behaves in these ways will not be followed for long.

BALANCE IN DEALING WITH OTHERS

Although no one likes a dictator, we do expect our leaders to exert their authority to keep things running smoothly. When they do not, everyone suffers.

Meg is the assistant night manager for a clothing store in the mall. One of her salespeople, Chrissy, often has friends visit during the evening. She talks with her visitors while Meg and Donna, the other salesperson, scurry to help customers and straighten the shelves. Although having visitors is against company policy, Meg is reluctant to say anything to Chrissy. "It's not worth the attitude she'll give me," Meg thinks. She does glare at Chrissy when her friends bring food into the store—they usually put it away fast after that. "At least they're careful around the clothes,"

Meg thinks. "Is it worth fighting over a few crumbs on the floor?"

There is a lot to be done at closing time each evening. Meg has posted a list of duties on the wall behind the cash register. Chrissy always manages to take so long rehanging clothing that Donna is stuck with the vacuuming. The big commercial machine is really heavy, so vacuuming is everybody's least-favorite job. Night after night, Donna seethes as she pushes the awkward appliance around, especially whenever she finds crumbs on the carpet.

Why doesn't Meg say anything to Chrissy? As the night manager, she certainly has the authority. But fearful of a conflict with Chrissy, she does nothing. Perhaps she hopes the problem will go away. Generally, problems get worse when we don't deal with

(Joe Duffy)

"Hold my calls!!!"

them. Nor is it fair to expect Donna and Chrissy to work it out themselves. This puts an unfair burden on Donna. It's the leader's job to resolve problems.

FACTOID:

In a survey of workers in a large organiza-tion, Dr. M. Millikin-Davies found their most common complaint was their supervisors' unwillingness "to confront problems and conflicts."

Those in charge sometimes worry that people won't like them if they use their authority. But followers won't like a leader who shirks her responsibility to take actions or make decisions that need to be made. Even in a participatory style of leadership like Richard's, the ultimate decision maker must be the leader. Letting things drift accomplishes nothing and makes everyone uncomfortable. If you've accepted a leadership role, you must be willing to *take charge.*

Being a leader is sometimes very difficult. Ability and hard work are not enough. Leadership requires skills in solving problems, sensitivity in dealing with others, and a willingness to make decisions and take action. But the key to great leadership is trust. A leader who does not earn our trust will soon be without followers.

The key to great leadership is trust. A leader who does not earn our trust will soon be without followers.

The leader must know, must know that he knows, and must be able to make it abundantly clear to those about him that he knows.

—Clarence Belden Randall

33

EXERCISE

It is not necessary to bite someone's head off to let them know you're in charge. A good leader can find a balance between being an ogre and a pushover. Describe how Meg could handle the two problems that she has with Chrissy. (You may make up a conversation between them if you want.)

2 WORKING WITH OTHERS TO GET WORK DONE

Felicia has worked part-time in a gift shop for two years. Her older sister also had worked there before going away to college, so Felicia feels knowledgeable about the business and very sure of herself. Mary, the owner, also has confidence in Felicia. She relies on Felicia as her most experienced part-timer.

One Saturday, Mrs. Ellis, a frequent customer, purchased a silver tray for an anniversary present and requested that it be gift wrapped. Felicia very carefully peeled off the price sticker before she wrapped the gift. After the customer had left, Janice, a fairly new sales clerk, quietly approached Felicia.

"I noticed that you threw the price sticker away. I'm so forgetful that I have to keep it where I can see it or else I start to wonder if I really *did* remove it. In the last shop I worked at, we had to stick it on the store copy of the receipt. That way we could double-check just by glancing at the receipt. That really helped me—maybe it would be good for you, too."

Felicia couldn't believe what she was hearing. "I didn't forget to remove the tag—I never do. I've been working here for two years and I've never once forgotten to remove the tag when the item is to be wrapped. What do you think I am... stupid?"

Janice was stunned. "Sorry. I was only trying to help."

Another clerk working in the back had heard Felicia's response. She whispered to Janice, "Don't worry. It's not your fault. You can't tell her anything. She's touchy that way. Just forget it."

A few months later, Mrs. Burton, a newlywed, asked Felicia's help in selecting a birthday present. She told Felicia she had a limited budget but hoped to find something special for her new mother-in-law. Felicia asked several questions about the mother-in-law's interests, and finally recommended a crystal vase. Mrs. Burton was thrilled to find that it was on sale, and that there was no charge for gift wrapping. "I'll certainly be sure to come in here whenever I need a present," she said.

(V. Harlow/Town & Country Nursery)

When you make a mistake at work, accept it and try to learn from it. If coworkers try to help by making suggestions so the same mistake won't happen again, treat their comments as constructive criticism and not as a personal attack on you or your efforts.

She returned just a few days later and asked for Felicia again. "I can't begin to describe how upset I was when my mother-in-law opened my gift and found the price still on the bottom of the vase. I was so embarrassed. You really should be more careful in the future."

Felicia was mortified, especially because Mary was close enough to hear the complaint. Mary came over and apologized and so did Felicia, but both suspected that Mrs. Burton would not be back to shop again soon. "Oh dear," said Felicia.

"Oh dear, indeed," said Mary. "I expected better of you, Felicia."

"Next time maybe I'll listen to what Janice and the others have to say," thought Felicia. "I guess I don't know everything."

CRITICISM CAN HELP YOU

Being criticized is almost always unpleasant, whether it is done by your friends, family, coworkers, or superiors. The important thing to remember is that criticism is not an attack on you, but on something that you did. If you can separate who you are from what you do, you will not feel the need to strike back or be defensive.

There's nothing dreadful about "being wrong"—everyone is at times. However, if you don't realize when you've made an error or if you stubbornly refused to accept it, you have fallen into an all-too-familiar snare.
>   —**J. W. McLean and William Weitzel**
>   *Leadership: Magic, Myth, or Method*

Acknowledging a mistake will not make your co-workers think less of you—as long as you also take steps to correct it. The purpose of criticism is, after all, to help someone improve. Your peers are often in the best position to know your weaknesses, as well as your strengths.

It really pays to listen, says the staff of Catalyst in *Making the Most of Your First Job.* Even if the criticism is not deserved, look for the kernel of truth that might be there. If you are able to consider what others want to tell you without being defensive, you have an opportunity to learn from them.

It is especially important for leaders to remain open to criticism. Catalyst says, "The higher you go, the less criticism you'll receive, the less indication you'll have as to how you're doing." Feedback from our

Feedback from our peers, or even our subordinates, can show us where we need to improve.

peers, or even our subordinates, can show us where we need to improve.

Criticism from a Superior

No matter how high you go in an organization, it is likely that you will still have someone above you. Part of his job is to supervise and advise you. Some of his advice may sting—criticism can indeed hurt. It will help to remember that your superior's intent is usually to teach and guide you. This guidance can only help you improve your performance and advance your career. So take it like a professional: don't interrupt, make excuses or blame someone else.

This does not mean that you should say nothing at all. Your response should indicate that you understand the points being made (or question further if you do not) and accept that you need to make an improvement. Beth Collins, senior planner for a clothing retail chain, says that a simple "OK" is the worst response.

The employer may think you are just giving lip service; that you hear, but not necessarily that you agree, or even understand. Your answer should show that you recognize that there is an issue that needs to be addressed. Ideally, I'd hope for a response that included how you plan to handle the same situation in the future.

EXERCISE

Constructive criticism can help us improve. Think of a time a teacher or other superior criticized your work. How did it help you to improve?

GIVING CRITICISM IS A DIFFICULT TASK

Jason worked nights at a diner that was a popular gathering place for high school students. Jason knew many of them because he himself had only graduated two years earlier. He now attended the local community college, but he hoped to transfer to a prestigious culinary college after completing his associate's degree the following year. He had always approached his job at the diner with a high degree of dedication and seriousness, and he had been rewarded for his efforts by a recent promotion to assistant manager.

One of his new responsibilities was supervising the servers. He knew everything about their tasks because he had been a waiter before his promotion. But he still sometimes felt uncomfortable telling a worker older than himself what to do. It was easier when the person was younger, as many of them were. In fact, most of the servers were still in high school.

Greg, a high school senior, had started working at the diner a few months ago. He was popular with the customers and his coworkers. His only fault was that he was occasionally late for his shift. One evening, Jason had to keep customers waiting because one waitress was out sick and Greg was late. Jason started feeling frantic and was just about to start taking the customers' orders himself when Greg walked in with several friends.

"Boy, have you got a lot of nerve!" Jason yelled. "We're going crazy while you just take your sweet time getting here. You do this all the time lately and you're taking advantage of everybody else. You must really think you're something! Well, I'll tell you what I think—I think your attitude and your work stinks. You can't even fill the salt and pepper shakers without spilling! You'll never make it in this business."

When Jason calmed down, he realized he had overreacted. His own panic about the backup in customers had triggered an unprofessional and uncalled-for response to the situation. Although he later apologized profusely to Greg, the damage was done. Greg worked his shift in a grim and stony silence, and everyone else avoided Jason for the entire evening.

Greg was certainly wrong to be late, and it was Jason's duty to tell him so. But not in front of others. When we criticize someone in front of others, even if in a *calm* manner, it will only make him defensive. An employee who feels he has been criticized in an unfair manner will often not accept the point of the criticism even if it is valid.

Focus on the problem, not the person. A comment like "You must really think you're something," is an attack on Greg, not his lateness. By publicly attacking the person, not the performance, Jason broke the top two rules for offering criticism. His later apologies could not undo the harm.

What should Jason have done? He should have waited until he was calmer and had all the facts. When we let emotion enter into our criticism, it will have a negative effect—on the person we are criticizing and on our ability to be clear about the problem. We may end up making blanket statements, like Jason's ("You

Focus on the problem, not the person.

do this all the time"). It is important to be fair and exact about the facts of the situation. How often was Greg late, really? And were there any extenuating circumstances this particular time? Jason did not even give Greg a chance to explain why he was late.

Stick to one issue. Don't bring up others, like the salt and pepper shakers. Leave the performance of other tasks to a later discussion. Also, try to balance the criticism with some praise and some encouragement. It must be clear to you and the worker that there is a way to improve the situation. Ask if there is anything you can do to help. Be ready to offer some concrete suggestions.

Offering criticism is one of the most difficult jobs of any leader.

It also helps to involve the worker in finding a solution to the problem. If lateness is truly part of a pattern, let the employee offer suggestions for solving his problem of getting to work on time. Alexander Welsh, author of *The Skills of Management,* suggests asking questions that will involve the worker, such as "How do you feel about the situation?" or "Is ___ going as well as you'd hoped?" By encouraging the worker to participate in finding a solution, you may lessen his resentment.

Offering criticism is one of the most difficult jobs of any leader. Always keep in mind that the purpose is to

Strong leaders win the loyal support of their followers because they share a common goal. Mohandas Gandhi's followers were motivated by his dedication to their common goal of freeing India from the rule of Great Britain without resorting to violence.

help the other person become more effective. These reminders will help you:

- ▶ Balance the criticism with praise.
- ▶ Focus on the performance, not the person.
- ▶ State the problem privately, in a reasonable tone of voice.
- ▶ Be specific about the facts of the matter. Make sure you have all the facts.
- ▶ Discuss what has to be done to keep the problem from happening again.

The greatest motivator is a shared goal.

By involving the other person in this process, you are more likely to get his cooperation to achieve the desired change. That, of course, is the ultimate goal of a good leader.

LEADERS MUST MOTIVATE THEIR FOLLOWERS

Leaders must have the cooperation of their followers. Someone who uses force or fear to get others to do what he wants is not a leader—he is a tyrant! Unfortunately, there are people in positions of leadership who do not know how to get others to cooperate.

The key is motivation. There must be something of value for the follower. The greatest motivator is a

LEADERSHIP RELIES ON SHARED GOALS

▶ Lincoln could not have pursued the Civil War if enough followers did not share his goals of preserving the Union and ending slavery.

▶ Martin Luther King Jr. was certainly a compelling preacher, but his followers would not have endured beatings, jail, and even death if they had not believed so strongly in the goal of civil rights for all.

▶ Gandhi's charisma was based on his inspirational example, but his followers also were motivated by their desire to free India from Britain's rule.

shared goal. People who agree with a goal will join to accomplish it.

Often the role of a leader is to define a goal in terms that show others the value of it to themselves. It may not be the same value the leader is seeking. Suppose a student wants to establish soda can recycling at her school. Some students welcome the opportunity to do something positive for the environment—they share her goal. Others can only be convinced to participate when it is pointed out that the deposit money will be added to the class trip fund.

EXERCISE

People are more apt to help if they understand and agree with a cause. Tell how you would convince someone to do one of the following:

1. Recycle their newspapers.

2. Volunteer at a soup kitchen.

3. Sell candy bars to raise money for the scholarship fund.

GAINING THE SUPPORT OF YOUR FOLLOWERS

A leader may gain and keep the support of followers by listening to their ideas. This builds a good relationship between the leader and follower. The leader earns the follower's support by indicating his trust in the follower's capabilities. His willingness to hear his followers' opinions shows respect and a desire to understand their feelings. People respond to those who make the effort to understand them.

People deserve to be recognized for the good work that they do—a simple "thank you," particularly in public, will build loyalty. When praise is specific, it also becomes a good teaching tool. It points out well-done elements that could carry over to other tasks.

The way to get a worker's best effort is to point out what he does well. When you comment on a worker's strong points, he learns what is expected and is likely to repeat the good work. It is easy to forget to give positive feedback—when work is done well, we tend to take it for granted. But positive feedback is essential to keeping a worker on the right track.
—Ann Holt, Hospital Administrator

By offering positive feedback first, you create a more receptive atmosphere in which to mention any areas that need improvement. Your followers will trust

(V. Harlow/Russell Library)

A good supervisor is patient when training a new employee. A boss also explains the job clearly, answers questions, and is diplomatic when criticizing a person's work abilities.

that you have their best interests at heart, and will tell them what they need to know. They will look to you for guidance—they realize that you can help them achieve the success they desire.

SUPERVISING OTHERS

Maggie Holahan works at a dry-cleaning store after school and on weekends. As an experienced worker, she is often asked to help train new employees.

"Some things should come naturally, like a pleasant attitude with the customers," says Maggie. "But I mention it anyway, and I try to set a good example. And I tell new people about the "uniform" we wear—navy shirts and khaki pants. The owner is pretty relaxed about it, as long as the shirt has a collar and is tucked in. It bugs me when the older kids come in to work on their college breaks with their shirttails hanging."

"There's a lot to remember when you work the counter," Maggie continues. "The computer alone takes getting used to. It will make several different kinds of slips—cleaning, laundering, tailoring. Each has its own menu of choices—prespotting, sizing, starch, box or hanger, crease or no crease, and so on. So while the new person watches me key the order in, I tell them in words what I am doing. Later, when I think they are ready, I'll have them do slips while I watch."

Most people want to feel good about themselves and what they do. A good supervisor helps others do their best by being clear about what to do and how to do it. Training a person takes time and effort. It shouldn't be left to chance, or left up to the worker to figure things out for himself. It is *your* responsibility to provide the direction he needs to do the job.

To waken interest and kindle enthusiasm is
the sure way to teach easily and successfully.
—Tyron Edwards

Begin simply, giving an overall explanation of the job. Explain any unfamiliar terms and equipment. Then break the job down into individual procedures. In *The Skills of Management,* Alexander Welsh notes that it is invaluable to demonstrate procedures. He suggests this pattern for getting the best results:

1. Break up any instruction into small units—one step of a procedure, or about one or two minutes of spoken instruction.

2. Pause at the end of each unit to let the learner react or catch up.

3. Check the learner's understanding. Answer any questions; clear up any confusion before going on. Demonstrate the step again if necessary.

4. When all steps have been explained and demonstrated, recap the whole procedure verbally.

5. Repeat the demonstration, one step at a time, explaining fully in detail each stage as you go.

6. Recap key stages verbally.

7. Have the learner try the procedure—talk him through it where necessary.

8. Point out errors as they occur in a noncritical manner.

9. Have the learner repeat the procedure if necessary.

Don't try to teach too many new procedures at once. Training should be an ongoing process. You probably didn't learn your job in a day. Make sure you show patience and a willingness to answer questions. Be realistic in your expectations.

HIGH EXPECTATIONS LEAD TO SUCCESS

Although it's important to be realistic about what others can accomplish, a leader can help by setting a good example and setting high standards. We've all known teachers who are sticklers about written work, for example. By forcing a student to rewrite an essay until it meets her standards, the teacher has helped the student produce a product of which he can be proud.

In order to help a worker meet standards, you

must monitor the worker's on-going performance, particularly at first. Only then will you truly know how to help the worker improve. If mistakes are made, they can be noted and corrected as they happen. If you wait to see the end-product, you may not be able to pinpoint what went wrong, and the worker may not be able to correct the problem without starting over.

Followers develop initiative when given a degree of freedom.

This does not mean that you have to constantly look over a worker's shoulder. Once you feel you have gotten the worker on the right track, you should give him more freedom. In *Frontiers of Leadership,* authors Michel Syrett and Clare Hogg advise trusting others to make decisions—even if this means having to live with some mistakes. People learn from their mistakes.

Syrett and Hogg further note that followers develop initiative when given a degree of freedom. They are willing to think for themselves, make and carry out decisions and take on more responsibility. It is still your job to define a clear set of "core responsibilities" to be carried out. But leaving room beyond that core expresses your desire for the worker to take some initiative. It also shows your confidence in his abilities. People generally try to live up to our expectations.

LEADING OTHERS TO SUCCESS

No matter how competent you are, you will often need to work with and rely on others. If they understand and share your goal, they will be motivated to do a good job. In fact, as a leader, you are in a position to help others do their very best. Your good example and high standards and expectations encourage their best efforts. Your careful training can get them on the right track and your praise and constructive criticism can help them improve. They will be willing to listen to you because you are willing to listen to them. By treating others fairly and telling them clearly and completely what you need them to do, you assure the best possible results. You cannot truly succeed without the success of others.

EXERCISE

In teaching someone how to do something new, we often take too much for granted. Even tasks that seem very simple to us may be confusing to someone else. On a piece of paper, outline the steps for performing a task you know how to do well. Then teach the task to someone who has

(Continued on page 56)

(Continued from page 55)

never done it before. You may find that you need to go into much more detail than the steps you outlined on paper. Try again, using the pattern for teaching a new procedure suggested by Alexander Welsh earlier in this chapter.

CHAPTER THREE
ORGANIZING A PROJECT COMES FIRST

Jared is an analyst for the marketing research division of Emco, an appliance manufacturer. His team's on-going assignments often involve general research on the competition's product lines. Special projects are initiated by the needs of other departments within Emco.

Recently, the small appliance division needed immediate research on a new hair dryer just marketed by their rival, Binder Company. Emco was developing a new hair dryer of its own. If its features were too similar to Binder's, Emco would delay production until additions or modifications could be made.

The manager of development explained the situation to Jared and asked him to get his team on the problem right away. Jared welcomed the challenge—usually his team's projects were so general and open-ended. Here was a way their work could make a direct contribution to the company. He wanted to jump-start the team.

"Listen up, people," he commanded his team. "Next project is Binder. Once again, they've gotten to market ahead of us. For once, I'd like us to be first. I don't know how they do it. But it's our job to find out. We've got a chance to make Emco stronger in the marketplace. I know you guys will do a great job—you're the best. So I'm counting on you to get it to me as soon as you can."

The team, with no specific knowledge of the hair dryer situation, assumed their assignment was another general examination of Binder's entire product line. Since they had on-going research on Binder in the files, they decided among themselves that Nick, one member of the team, would update the files and prepare a report. The rest of them were working on other things that seemed more important.

When Jared checked several days later on their progress, he was devastated to find out that only Nick was working on it and that he had barely begun. "Where's an assessment of Binder's new dryer? Why hasn't someone conducted a survey of households on the desired features in a handheld dryer? What's the matter with you guys?"

"What new dryer?" asked Nick. "Nobody said anything about any new dryer. How were we supposed to know?"

In order to do a good job, people need to know *what* they are trying to do and *why* they are trying to do it. A leader has the responsibility to explain the purpose and goals of the work he assigns to the members of his team. After all, they are the ones whose efforts will help achieve those goals.

Goals must be clearly defined; they should not be too general. Don't just say, "Do your best" or "Take care of it" or "As soon as possible." In communicating the goal to his team, a leader must be as concrete as possible about what tasks must be done to reach the goal. It is important to be realistic about the amount of effort that will be needed for each task and set a reasonable deadline for completing the project.

For example, the following statement by the manager of the employee benefits division to his staff is not specific enough:

Our goal is to inform employees about the choices for a new health plan.

A better goal also would state how and when this is to be accomplished:

By September 12, all employees must be

> A leader has the responsibility to explain the purpose and goals of the work he assigns to the members of his team.

informed about the differences in the benefits and costs of the three proposed health plans. Our department will provide information sessions in Conference Room B from 11 A.M. to 12 noon every Thursday from now until September 12.

The benefits staff can now readily see that they will need to prepare and present these information sessions to achieve their goal.

Goals must be specific, have a timetable, and be achievable. Goals that are too ambitious will discourage those who fear they cannot reach them. Goals that are too easy may breed carelessness or boredom. Good goals "stretch" the worker and encourage him to put forth his best effort.

We... conclude that, in general, moderately difficult goals seem to result in higher performance than easy or extremely difficult goals.

Charles C. Manz and Henry Sims,
*SuperLeadership: Leading Others
to Lead Themselves*

If goals are not clearly set, the project is likely to be completed unsatisfactorily. If people don't know *what* they are supposed to do, they can't possibly do it. Don't count on them asking questions—instead they may just guess, and not always correctly. And if people don't know *why* they are to do something, they may not care enough to do it well. It's human nature—if the leader doesn't care enough about the project to properly explain it, why should anyone care about doing it?

TEAM PARTICIPATION IN DEVELOPING THE PROJECT

Once a project's overall goal has been determined and communicated to the team, it is often possible to involve the members in decisions concerning the development of the project. This participation depends on the situation, the experience of the team and the difficulty of the project. Participation has two benefits:

1. Brainstorming sessions can yield many good ideas about how to proceed, who should do which assignments and when individual tasks should be completed.

2. The more you involve your team, the harder they are likely to work.

Effective motivators know that the involvement of those who will be part of the group trying to reach those goals is crucial to the outcome.
>   —J. W. McLean and William Weitzel,
>   *Leadership: Magic, Myth, or Method*

J. W. McLean and William Weitzel surveyed thousands of workers to ask specifically what motivated them the most. Strangely enough, money and job security were not at the top of the list. The results showed that workers most valued being appreciated, followed closely by "being an insider." Being an insider may simply mean knowing the goals and purpose of the work to be done or being kept informed about company developments. But it is workers who are included in some of the decisions about goals and assignments who may feel most *appreciated*.

Many other researchers have come to the conclusion that workers want to feel a part of what they do. In the introduction to the new edition of *The 100 Best Companies to Work for in America,* authors Robert Levering and Milton Moskowitz say "more employee participation" is a key area of positive change in the 1990s.

The top companies all received the highest ratings (four or five stars) for "pride" and "openness/fairness." A high pride rating indicates that employees feel a direct connection with their company's product or service. In companies rated high in openness, two-way communication—information to employees and suggestions and criticisms *from* employees—is the norm.

FACTOID:

Ice-cream maker Ben and Jerry's rates high in pride and openness. Company meetings are held every three months to keep employees up-to-date. Some of the meetings are scheduled for midnight for the benefit of the late shift; other workers attend in their pajamas.

GETTING ORGANIZED

Although involving the team may have many rewards, it is ultimately the responsibility of the leader to organize the project. It will not organize itself, and it cannot be left to chance.

"I really hated working on group projects in high school," says college freshman Alicia Barron. "Nobody was ever in charge, like that was against

Employees appreciate being "part of the team." Ice-cream makers, Ben Cohen and Jerry Greenfield, schedule company meetings so that employees from all shifts are given the opportunity to attend and participate.

the rules or something. So nothing ever got done until the last minute, or two people ended up doing the same part or a part didn't get done at all. And you know that certain people always did most of the work, even though everybody got the same grade.

"I really like the system they have here, though,"

Alicia continues. "In my honors seminar, I work with the same three other students on projects all semester long. We rotate the leader position with each new project. The leader decides how the work should be divided, who should do which parts and when. He or she is usually extremely fair because otherwise we'll get 'em back on the next project."

Good order is the foundation of all good things.
—Edmund Burke

Being the leader may not be as simple as Alicia describes it, especially if the project is a complicated one. It helps to first organize your own thinking about the project. What are the individual tasks that need to be done in order to reach the project's goal? Who will do each task? When will each task need to be completed?

The more tasks that are involved in a project, the more organizational skills you will need. Stephanie Winston, author of *The Organized Executive,* suggests that you organize the individual tasks into their proper order. Some tasks have to be performed one at a time, with each being finished before the next can be started. Sometimes several tasks can be handled at once. It depends on the nature of the project and the individual tasks.

The next step, suggests Winston, is to set a deadline for each task. Always schedule some extra time into the plan—problems are bound to come up. Finally, assign the tasks to yourself and others. Check that each person knows his or her assignments and the deadlines.

In summary, organizing a project has five basic steps:

Always schedule some extra time into the plan—problems are bound to come up.

1. State the goal and final deadline.

2. List all the tasks that must be done.

3. Put those tasks in the proper order.

4. Set a deadline for each task.

5. Assign tasks to yourself and others.

EXERCISE

Use the five basic steps listed above to describe how you would organize a car wash.

DELEGATING RESPONSIBILITY

The ultimate goal of a leader is to get the very best contribution from *all* members of the team. This includes the leader! At times, the leader will be the best person to do a particular task; if not, he should delegate the task to someone else.

Responsibility walks hand in hand with capacity and power.

—Josiah Gilbert Holland

Laura is the president of her church youth group. Part of their outreach program is providing holiday gifts for needy children. The whole congregation participates, but the youth group organizes the drive, wraps the gifts and delivers them.

Each child's name, age, gender, and size have to be recorded on a master list and on an index card. The cards are available to any member of the congregation who wishes to buy a gift for a child. Usually the index cards are written by hand, but Laura thinks that the master list information could be produced as stick-on labels by computer. Since Mark, her vice president, seems more knowledgeable about computers than she is, she asks him if that's something he can do.

"Sure," says Mark. "I'm great on the computer. I'll type the master list, tell the computer to produce the labels and then stick them down on index cards." Laura tells him generally what she needs, and he promises to have the cards in time for the congregation's main service on Sunday.

When he brings the completed cards to the service, Laura is thrilled—until she checks them. There was no "boy" or "girl" information. Some names could be either, like "Alex." Mark is willing to add that information by hand, but valuable time will be lost. Many members of the congregation had planned to pick up a card at the coffee hour following the service.

"It's not your fault, Mark. I didn't think it through and tell you all you needed to know," said Laura. "I was just so thrilled to get someone to do it on the computer."

Laura was on the right track when she asked someone else to do a task she was not comfortable doing. And perhaps Mark was the best person for that task. But Laura forgot to give him some important information. When delegating responsibility, be clear about what you need.

WHEN TO DELEGATE

A person in charge may delegate work to others for many reasons. Like Laura, there may be a task that someone else would be better able to do. Or perhaps the leader realizes that she has so many responsibilities in overseeing the project that others will have to take on many of the tasks. And why not, as long as she can find someone who can do a task as well as she herself could?

Ask yourself which of your activities could be done by somebody else—adequately, as well as you can, or even better than you can do it.
—**Alexander N. Welsh,**
The Skills of Management

A leader must decide what the *best* use of his time will be.

The problem with delegating for many leaders is thinking that no one else can do the task as well. This may indeed be the case but that should not necessarily stop a leader from delegating the task if somebody else can do an *adequate* job. A leader must decide what the *best* use of his time will be. Perhaps there are many other aspects of the project that only the leader can handle. In this case, he may need to delegate less-demanding tasks to others—even if they cannot do as good a job as he himself could do.

HOW TO DELEGATE

Telling someone what to do requires a balanced approach. A hesitant tone can lead the other person to be unsure of your intention; an arrogant tone can lead to resentment. A feeling of mutual trust produces the best results. You trust someone on your team to do the task to the best of his ability; that person trusts you to provide the support he will need to do it. This includes supplying all the information and materials needed and adequate time to complete the task.

The key to delegation is the word entrust. When you delegate, you entrust the entire matter to the other person, along with suffi-cient authority to make necessary decisions. This is quite a different thing from saying, "Just do what I tell you to do."

—Edwin C. Bliss,
*Getting Things Done:
The ABC's of Time Management*

The information given should be as specific and detailed as possible. Don't assume that other people understand what you want, even if they don't ask questions. They may hesitate out of fear—they don't want to seem stupid or be a bother. If possible, write down the assignment. The clearer you are, the easier their job will be—and the better the results. The purpose in delegating is to save time and effort. The task may have to be redone if you're misunderstood.

ASSIGNING TASKS

Rebecca explains how her promotion to a leadership position has challenged her.

"When I was first promoted, I was thrilled," says Rebecca. "Then reality set in. I used to just do what I was told. Now my boss comes to me with a project and a deadline and the rest is up to me. Well, not *just* me. I have a great team. But it's my job to make the best use of them. The hardest part is giving out assignments.

"At first, when I didn't know my team very well, I would list the tasks that needed to be done on a sheet of paper," Rebecca continues. "Then I'd have everybody indicate whether they were strong or weak in that kind of activity. The problem was, they were not always realistic. Usually they underestimated themselves. But I didn't know if they really thought a task was too hard or if they just didn't want too much work. Others overrated their strengths and I didn't know until it was too late that they were in over their heads."

"As I came to know their abilities better," continues Rebecca, "I felt more comfortable making assignments. But there are still problems. Some parts of a project are more involved than others and take more time. It takes a lot of experience to gauge the amount of effort a particular task will take. If I miscalculate, somebody is going to be overburdened and angry. I actually keep a log of past assignments: who did it, how long it took, how well it was done. It helps me to be more realistic about how long it takes to do certain types of jobs. It has also helped me build a profile of each member of the team: their strengths and weaknesses, their styles of working and their preferences."

"I can't always give them what they want," concludes Rebecca, "but I do avoid favoritism—an assignment should be based strictly on a person's ability to perform the job."

As Rebecca has found, one of the most difficult

responsibilities of a leader is choosing the right person for a particular task. A leader should never simply assign a complicated, multitask project to a team without sorting out who will do what. Sometimes the choice is obvious: a member of the team has demonstrated a clear and superior ability for a type of work.

In other cases, the leader may consult with his team to see if there are preferences for assignments. But the leader must still use his judgment as to which worker is best suited to a particular task. He will need to be familiar with his team's talents and skills to make a good match. Some people work best at assignments that are technical in nature. Others shine in situations that involve interacting with other people. Certain tasks require a great deal of patience; others require an immediate reaction. A leader must really know the job as well as the person.

Responsibility is the thing people dread most of all. Yet it is the one thing in the world that develops us, gives us manhood or womanhood fibre.

—Frank Crane

A GOOD LEADER IS OBJECTIVE

It may be natural to give the best assignment, or the easiest schedule or the most credit to certain individuals. Perhaps they fully deserve your good attentions. But it is possible that you are being unfair to others who also may deserve a break. Avoid even the appearance of playing favorites. Vary assignments and schedules in a way that is fair to all. Avoid loading the least attractive tasks on the same person. If there are a number of those types of tasks throughout the project, a rotating schedule can be used from the start. Everyone can take a turn in doing the undesirable tasks.

Don't make judgments about people automatically, or on feeling alone. Always question your objectivity. Do the facts back up your opinion? Is the highly likable, outgoing Steve really the best person for this particular task? Perhaps, but you may be overlooking a quiet but more competent worker. You also need to be aware of your own blind spots and prejudices. People are individuals, and they deserve to be treated as such.

Also, everyone deserves a second chance. Perhaps there is someone who once did a poor job for you. Be sure you view his current capabilities objectively. There may have been circumstances that interfered

(Joe Duffy)

with his earlier performance. It's important that you have a realistic understanding of the pressures and needs of others. A good leader wants to know all

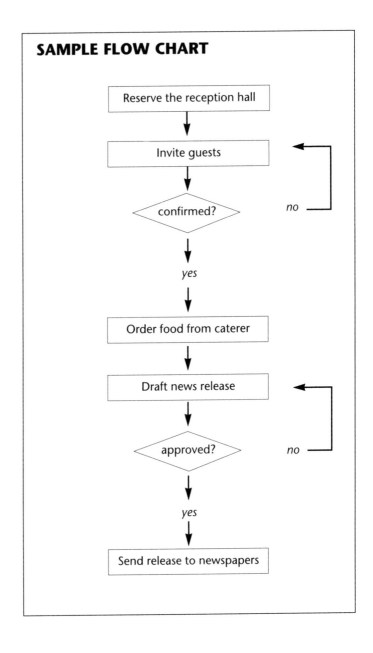

SAMPLE FLOW CHART

Reserve the reception hall

↓

Invite guests

↓

confirmed?   *no*

yes

↓

Order food from caterer

↓

Draft news release   *no*

↓

approved?

yes

↓

Send release to newspapers

about the members of his team—their strengths as well as their weaknesses—so that he can lead them effectively.

CHARTING YOUR COURSE

When a project requires the completion of a number of tasks, a chart can help the team to visualize the course they will need to follow.

A **flow chart** shows each task in sequence. In order to make a flow chart, first make a list of tasks that will have to be done to reach your project's goal. Then put the tasks in the order in which they must be done. Use *boxes* to show tasks and *diamonds* to indicate decision points. These diamond checkpoints can keep you from going ahead when you may actually need to go back to a previous task. Here is a sample chart for planning a reception for an honored guest.

The diamonds show points where things might get held up: invitees who have not confirmed their attendance and the approval of your news release. In the first case, if all confirmations are not in, you cannot yet order the food. In the second case, your superior may ask you to redraft the news release before you send it to the newspapers. The side arrows send you back to the step that will need to be redone.

In summary, to create a flow chart:

1. At the top of a piece of paper, write the first task to be done. Put a box around it.

2. Draw a line or arrow down and list the next task, putting a box around it.

3. Continue listing each task in sequence, with arrows flowing from the previous task to the new one.

4. Use a diamond shape to indicate any point at which a decision, confirmation, or approval must be made before the next task can be done. If so, use side arrows to point back to the step that needs to be redone.

Although a basic flow chart does not indicate who will do each task or when it is due, you can add this information to the task box. The flow chart can be a very useful tool in organizing a project.

GANTT CHARTS

A flow chart shows tasks to be done in sequence. Sometimes tasks go on simultaneously. A simple horizontal chart, called a *Gantt,* can show the timing of both sequential and simultaneous tasks. Since this type of chart shows the relative amount of time allo-

SAMPLE GANTT CHART

Task	Assigned	2/11	2/12	2/13	2/14	2/15	2/18	2/19	2/20	2/21	2/22
Reserve room	Ellen	▓									
Send memos	Max	▓									
Develop activities	Jane	▓	▓								
Prepare activity sheets	Jane/Max			▓	▓	▓					
Reserve equipment	Ellen			▓							
Print materials	Ellen						▓	▓			
Collate folders	Ellen									▓	
Conduct workshop	Jane/Max										▓

cated to each task, it is also called a *time/task analysis.*

The first column down the left side of the chart lists the tasks in the order that they will be performed. All tasks, including relatively simple ones, should be listed.

The next column is filled in with the name of the person assigned to the task.

A person may be assigned more than one task. These assignments may be provisional at first. As you analyze how much time is required for each task, you may need to shift assignments.

The top row of the chart is a timeline from the project's start date to its end date. The timeline can be expressed in days, weeks, or months—whichever is appropriate. A horizontal bar connects the beginning and ending dates of an individual task. Take a look at the chart for planning a workshop. By looking at the chart, you can tell which tasks will go on simultaneously. Some related activities even overlap: preparing activity sheets can begin while some workshop activities are still being developed. The chart also shows that equipment should not be reserved until all activities have been planned.

TAKE TIME TO ORGANIZE

Organizing a project always begins with setting a goal and communicating it to others who will be involved. Remember that their efforts will be related to their understanding of the goal: specific goals with clear targets and set timetables are best.

Next, decide what tasks will be necessary to reach the project's goal, and be clear about when each

(Courtesy: Kelly Services)

Computer graphics and charts can be very useful and time saving when planning a main project. Graphics also enable people to visualize the course that needs to be followed to achieve the final goal.

must be completed. Delegate these tasks to others according to their interests and abilities. Be fair and objective; if possible, involve them in decisions about their assignments. A chart of assignments can help them understand the project and how their tasks will contribute to achieving it.

EXERCISE

Create a Gantt chart for a team of three to prepare and present an oral report. Use lined paper to show the timing of five or more tasks for this project.

CHAPTER FOUR
COMPLETING A PROJECT

"**P**lanning the sales conference is a big responsibility, but I am confident that you'll do a good job," said Tom's boss. "You've got a great team, and I'll assist you in any way I can. Now let's sit down and discuss the focus of the conference. I'll leave planning the actual agenda to you and your team."

But when Tom returned to his department, he began to worry. There were so many things to do to plan the sales conference. He called his team together to tell them the news. "Our goal is to plan a three-day sales conference to be held June 12 through the 14th in Omaha. The agenda will focus on developing an international market."

The team immediately began brainstorming, generating a long list of tasks that would need to be accomplished over the coming months. Eventually,

Tom scheduled a meeting for the following week and sent them back to their regular duties.

Over the next several days, Tom worked on creating an assignment chart to present at the next meeting. It wasn't too difficult deciding who would do what.

His team had planned a half-day workshop two months ago. He had been impressed with his team's cooperation and had come to know their individual capabilities. The in-house workshop had gone extremely well. Tom was sure that was the reason his boss, Mr. Kane, had chosen them for this new responsibility.

"The difference is this time it's three days," he thought. "We have to take into account transportation, hotel arrangements, outside speakers, catering, and recreation. I'm sure we're forgetting some things. I'd better get the team started on all of this right away. That way, when something else pops up, we'll have time to work it in."

At the meeting the following week, Tom unveiled his Gantt chart. The column of tasks seemed to go on forever. "We're going to be really busy around here," Tom admitted. "Let me know if any of you have any conflicts."

People diligently began making notes in daybooks and pocket calendars.

"I have a problem," said Phil." If I do all my assignments for this project that are due in the next two weeks, I won't be able to get any of my regular work done."

"This is hard," said Hilary. "I keep losing my place on the chart. My name is all over the place. I'm afraid I'm going to miss one of my assignments."

Ed agreed. "I'm not sure I can follow the chart, either. I think this may be too big a project to have just one chart. I'd like to suggest that we 'chunk' the tasks. Put all the planning tasks in one chunk—planning the agenda, choosing the speakers, researching recreational opportunities. Then chunk the logistical tasks, like sending out notices, making travel and hotel arrangements, and booking the speakers."

"Great idea, Ed," said Tom. "You and I are responsible for the planning tasks, so I'll make a chart for us. But the logistical tasks will have to be broken down even further. I'll work on a new kind of chart that will help each person see his or her chunk of work more easily. And I'll reconsider the due dates for some of the assignments. Thank you all for your honesty, and you, Ed, for your idea."

Tom was fortunate that his team spoke up. If they hadn't voiced their concerns, Tom would have assumed everything was okay. But due dates must be realistic to take into account other work that must be done, and to allow for delays, problems, and corrections. And a chart that is too complicated to follow is no help at all.

As the leader, Tom needs to provide the team with a clear way to follow their tasks through the project. For example, Hilary's basic responsibility—to secure the hotel—involved three separate tasks that were indeed "all over" the Gantt chart. Selecting a hotel is one of the very first things that needed to be done, but actually booking it would not come until later. Final confirmation on the number of rooms would be months away. These tasks were, therefore, separated on the Gantt chart.

TASK-BY-LEVEL CHARTING

Tom wants to create a chart that will list all of these tasks close together. The tasks are presented in a chunk so that each team member can easily identify their specific responsibilities. The kind of chart Tom is looking for is a "tasks-by-levels" chart, designed by Stephanie Winston, author of The Organized Execu-

tive. In this type of chart, tasks are divided by levels and put into columns:

Although each of Hilary's tasks is in a separate column, she can see them by reading across the top line of the chart. Study the chart below, which was adapted from Stephanie Winston's design. You'll notice that:

- *Level 1 tasks* go in the first column. These tasks can be carried out first because they do not depend on any other tasks. For example, Hilary can gather hotel brochures.

- *Level 2 tasks* depend on the completion of one or more Level 1 tasks. In this example, once research has been done, Hilary can book the hotel that has the facilities her company needs. This task would be listed in the second column.

- *Level 3 tasks* cannot be done until the completion of one or more Level 2 tasks. In this instance, Hilary would wait to make a final confirmation until she had a list of attendees. This task would be listed in the last column.

The tasks-by-level chart makes it easier for workers to see their various assignments. It also helps them to see the relationships and dependencies between tasks, and the order in which they must be done. When a project is long-term and multitasked, chunking tasks in this way can help everyone keep track of their assignments.

SAMPLE TASKS-BY-LEVELS CHART

Level 1			Level 2			Level 3		
Due	**To**	**Task**	**Due**	**To**	**Task**	**Due**	**To**	**Task**
10/7	HJ	Gather hotel brochures	11/25	HJ	Book hotel	3/30	HJ	Confirm hotel
10/9	DL	Estimate of attendees	12/15	DL	Send notices to attendees	4/3	DL	Select menus
10/11	FB	Contact travel agent for information	4/1	FB	Make travel arrangements	4/9	FB	Reserve golf course
11/30	PG	Book speakers	4/1	PG	Order audio-visual equipment	6/11	PG	Supervise equipment installation

EXERCISE

The Key Club is planning a carnival to benefit the local children's hospital. Put the list of tasks below into three levels. You will have three tasks in each level. Remember that Level 2 tasks cannot begin until certain Level 1 tasks have been accomplished, and Level 3 tasks depend on the completion of some Level 2 tasks.

Set up game booths; Get permit for a town playground; Prepare food, Advertise in newspaper; Order food supplies; Plan games; Hire amusement ride company; Rent food tent; Purchase prizes

MONITORING THE TEAM'S PROGRESS

Sarah is the editor in chief of the Lincoln High School yearbook. She is bright, dedicated, and has a talented staff. The only problem seems to be deadlines.

"I've worked on the past three yearbooks," says Sarah, "and we never missed a single deadline before. This year we've really had a lot of problems. I try to keep after everybody, but there's so much to keep track of. Sometimes it isn't our fault—a computer virus destroyed eight pages of the senior section. But some situations were just somebody not doing their job on time."

"Even so," continues Sarah, "I always feel like it's my fault. I wish I could figure out a way to monitor each and every task. Because of all the late fees we had to pay for those missed deadlines, our budget ran over. We had planned to use spot color for headlines in every section. Now we can only afford it in the Senior Life section. We're all so disappointed."

Sarah's disappointment is understandable. She has devoted so much time to planning and producing the yearbook. Because of late fees, it won't have the look she had envisioned.

In business, missing a deadline can be very costly and have serious consequences. The leader must find a way to keep track of the various tasks that need to be done, and when they need to be completed. It is important to not rely on memory. Some *system* of monitoring the progress of each task is essential. As the person in charge, choose the system that fits your situation.

Some system of monitoring the progress of each task is essential.

NOTEBOOK TRACKING

If a project is relatively simple, a notebook can be used to track its various tasks. Decide on the order in which tasks will need to be done. Assign each task a page in your notebook in sequence. Record the details that apply to the task—who has been assigned, the deadline for that task and a date you intend to check on its progress. Deadlines and dates for progress checks should also be recorded on your calendar. Here is how a notebook page would look:

Task: Order food

To: Margaret

Due: February 16

Progress check: February 9

_____ *I have entered these dates in my calendar*

_____ *I have made the progress check*

_____ *Task is completed*

EXERCISE

Make two more notebook pages patterned on the one above. Use any two tasks from Tom's sales conference tasks-by-levels chart depicted earlier in this chapter.

Remember to set a progress check date that provides enough time to solve problems and make any necessary corrections.

CALENDARS

No matter what system you choose to monitor your team's progress, you will always need to rely on a calendar to prompt you. For example, flow charts, Gantts or tasks-by-levels charts all need to be backed up by recording due dates on a calendar. If you made a task/assignment chart in the project's planning stage, post it where all team members can see it. This will help them follow the sequence of tasks. But the chart alone will not help you, as leader, check their progress and monitor deadlines. You will need a checking system.

Often a large wall calendar or month-at-a-glance poster will be sufficient for monitoring a simple project. Enter each task and the name of the assigned person on the task's due date. Use a different colored marker for each person. As each task is completed, cross it off with a bold black diagonal line. This will make it evident which tasks remain to be done. The unmarked squares are your prompts to check on the status of those tasks.

If there are many tasks in a project, you will need to set actual dates for progress checks; record these dates on your own desk calendar. These "check dates" should be well enough in advance of the actual due dates to allow time for correcting any problems. If corrections need to be made, enter a "recheck" date on your desk calendar.

It is important, however, to avoid "overmanaging" the project. If you are always looking over your worker's shoulders, they may not do anything without reminders or help from you. The progress checks are simply for your overall control and to reinforce *their* accountability.

TEAM MEETINGS

A leader may choose to monitor a project and check on progress toward deadlines by scheduling regular team meetings. The members report on the status of

(V. Harlow/Vinal Regional Vocational Technical School, Middletown, CT)

Team meetings are important to monitor progress toward the completion of any complex project. As the team leader, you evaluate the members' progress and resolve any unanticipated problems so the deadline can be met on time.

their assigned tasks. Everyone has the opportunity to see where everyone else is on the project.

A good discussion...is fundamentally a cooperation. It progresses toward some understanding.

—Randolph Stillman Bourne

The leader can check on team members' progress and help them deal with any problems. More supplies may need to be ordered. If a task is not producing the result needed, then the team may help develop another plan. Priorities can be set and adjustments may be made to the schedule.

An added benefit of meetings is that they can clear up any misconceptions about the project. Someone's question may help the whole team come to a better understanding of an issue. Meetings also provide the opportunity for a leader to probe the team's feelings about the project. Perhaps they are becoming overwhelmed by the workload. It may be time for the leader to add more staff. Often workers can be "borrowed" from another department for brief periods.

FACTOID:

Interaction between leaders and subordinates results in greater group output. Several studies have shown that managers who received subordinate feedback were more effective on the job.

The value of two-way feedback—leader to subordinate and subordinate to leader—is undeniable. A good leader will be sure to interact with his subordinates throughout the course of a project. Meetings are a prime opportunity for such interaction. At meetings, things may come out that a leader could not possibly pick up by simply monitoring deadlines. The disadvantage is that meetings take time. Many leaders, therefore, use meetings only infrequently, and in combination with one of the other methods for checking progress described earlier in this chapter.

A good leader will be sure to interact with his subordinates throughout the course of a project.

QUESTIONS FOR CHECKING A TEAM'S PROGRESS

1. Will the team meet the project's deadlines?

2. Is the team completing all of its work, including other tasks unrelated to the project?

3. Is the supply of materials adequate for the team's needs?

4. Are enough team members available to complete the project in a timely manner?

EVALUATING PROGRESS

As a leader follows the progress of her team toward the project's goal, there will be times when she may have to point out faults and suggest corrections. But her attitude should be one of guidance and support, not scolding or punishment. Her purpose is to evaluate the team's efforts and to make adjustments as necessary. Her objective is to move the team toward the project's goal.

People need to know how they are getting along and what progress they are making.... Often, the most effective way to speed up what is being done is to give recognition and commendation to those who deserve it, and thus spur them to greater effort.

—Ray A. Killian *Leadership on the Job*

ASSESSING THE PROJECT

"I don't think I could ever go through that again," said Adam. "It was certainly a worthwhile goal, but the process of getting there was a killer."

97

Adam was referring to his company's Work Weekend. Every fall the entire company put aside a weekend to make repairs on houses of senior citizens. Adam was glad he worked for a company with a social conscience, but this year the job of coordinating the project had fallen to his department. They had nearly gone crazy organizing the weekend, and many things had gone wrong.

"There has to be a better way," he thought. "It's a good thing we're having a team meeting tomorrow." Carrie, his department head, had called the meeting to assess the department's handling of the Work Weekend.

"The first thing I'd like to say is thank you all so much," Carrie began. "We weatherized and repaired over 30 homes. But we did have a lot of problems that I'd like to talk about now. Even though another department will rotate into the coordinator's position next year, I still feel we can offer them the benefit of our experience. And believe it or not, the troubles we had with the Work Weekend may carry over into other areas in our department. So let's see where things went wrong."

Carrie had come to the meeting armed with the original flow chart she had developed many weeks ago. Looking at the chart immediately triggered Adam's memory.

"I was in charge of purchasing supplies," he said, "but I had to have Mr. Cole sign every purchase order. Tracking him down wasn't always easy. If I left the P. O. on his desk, he might not get it back to me for several days. Maybe he could designate a second person to act on these special requests—someone who's more available."

Carrie told Adam she thought that was a good idea and promised to forward his suggestion to Mr. Cole. The team continued to study the steps of the flow chart to see where there had been lapses or bottle-necks. They brainstormed solutions to many of the problems. One major result was the institution of a new procedure: a detailed questionnaire would be sent to next year's homeowners. Better information would make it possible to order the correct supplies in advance, thus saving extra trips to the hardware store once repairs began.

By the time the meeting was over, the team felt satisfied that they had done a good job of assessing their project and suggesting improvements for the future. They also felt that Carrie appreciated their efforts, however imperfect. More importantly, she had demonstrated her respect for their opinions.

Not all assessments involve a meeting. Sometimes the team leader prepares a written report for his superior. In that case, the leader will often consult with his team in drafting the report. Or he may ask the team members to respond to a questionnaire about their experience with the project. The process of answering the questions or preparing a report may clarify situations for the writers as well as the intended readers.

When a project is completed, there is a tendency to breathe a sigh of relief, no matter what the outcome. But in order for a team to improve, it must look at the project objectively. Many small, seemingly minor glitches in a project may add up to a less-than-satisfactory result. In addition, problems that are not corrected are bound to occur in another project.

STEPS TO A SUCCESSFUL PROJECT

Planning a project is only the first step. A leader must then make sure that the necessary tasks are carried out by his team in a timely manner. If the project is complex, chunking tasks into levels before charting them is helpful. Deadlines can be recorded on large wall calendars or month-at-a-glance posters. A leader should also record progress "check dates" on his desk calendar. By checking on tasks well before they are due, adjustments can be made and problems solved before it is too late.

One way to check progress is by scheduling team meetings. Status reports help everyone to know how the project is progressing. Two-way feedback results in greater effectiveness by all members of the team. Positive feedback by the leader generally encourages team members to increase their efforts toward the project's goal.

Once the goal has been reached, it is important to identify areas that can be improved in the future. Objective assessments and recommendations for improvements are the final steps in any project.

EXERCISE

Almost everyone has worked at some time on a project that—while good-intentioned—did not turn out as planned and organized. Maybe it was a school car wash, or a field trip that you and other students had a hand in organizing, or a group presentation for history class. Evaluate one of these

(Continued on page 102)

(Continued from page 101)

past projects and identify what went right and what could have been done better. Could the use of organizational tools such as Gantt- or Flow-charts increased the chances of success? Did the project suffer because of poor communication and infrequent team meetings? Write a short analysis of the project with suggestions to how you improve its success for future students.

CHAPTER FIVE
LEARNING TO LEAD

"This is making me crazy," thought Dan as he sat staring out of his office window.

"I've won the Art Director's Club design award twice, and this company won't even give me a chance at the *assistant* art director's position. I can't for the life of me figure out what's wrong."

Dan had majored in graphic design at a prestigious art college on the East Coast. When he graduated, he was thrilled to land a job as a graphic designer for a book publisher. Designing book covers combined his love of art with two secondary loves—reading and computer technology. His schooling had prepared him for computer design, a requirement in the publishing industry. Everyone had thought Dan was on the fast track to success, especially Dan himself.

But he was passed over when the assistant art director's position became vacant. One of the other designers, a new employee named Kristen, commiserated with him over his disappointment. "You're very talented. I think they're going to be sorry they didn't move you up," she said. "Do you even have a clue why they passed you by?"

"Mike thinks it's the way I look, but that's too stupid to be it. I mean, who cares these days? I've always worn jeans and Birkenstocks and I always will. It shouldn't matter how I dress, as long as I can do the work."

But when Dan finally worked up his courage to approach Jack, the art director, he was shocked to find out that his appearance had indeed been a major factor in the company's decision not to advance Dan. "It's not just talent, Dan," said Jack. "The assistant art director is a leadership position. The company was worried you were too young anyway, and your appearance just confirmed that opinion. I'm sorry."

"This is so unbelievably unfair," sputtered Dan. "And why didn't somebody say something?"

"I did," said Jack. "Maybe I was too casual about how I said it, but don't you remember my comment the day you wore that tie-dyed shirt to the editors'

(Joe Duffy)

"Ed is going to ruin 'dress-down Friday' for all of us."

meeting? And the time you tinted your hair? Your response both times was just a smile. I figured you were happy to be a designer and had no plans to move up. That's the message you were sending with your appearance. And I don't think we were reading you wrong—if you had really wanted to be in a leadership position, you would have made an effort to look the part."

DRESS FOR SUCCESS

Whether we like it or not, appearance does matter. People will generally be more confident in someone who is professionally dressed and well groomed. Dressing professionally does not necessarily mean wearing a dress or suit and tie. It depends on the position, the organization, and even in which part of the country the organization is located.

Certain creative fields, such as music, art, and advertising, are thought to be more accepting of individual expression in clothing style. But Bradley G. Richardson, in his book *Jobsmarts for Twentysomethings,* offers this advice: "Just remember, it's the work that shows how creative you are, not how you dress."

Dress-for-success books recommend dressing as well or better than the industry standard if you want respect. Even if a workplace is casual, someone who aspires to a leadership position will make sure he dresses appropriately. In some places this may simply mean dressing in a collared shirt tucked into neat jeans. Take your cue from workers who are in the level you hope to achieve. Also, if your company has "dress-down Fridays," don't overdo the casual look if you are serious about a leadership position.

You may feel it shouldn't matter. You are the same

person under whatever clothes you wear. But like it or not, appearance can inspire confidence—and inspiring confidence is *your* job if you want to lead.

BODY ADORNMENTS

People have preconceived ideas about how leaders should look. In the real world (that is, the workplace) this does not usually include sporting attention-getting body adornments. Indulge in obvious tattoos at your own peril. Facial piercing should be limited to the ears and limit the number or earrings in general. Again, note what is acceptable by observing people in positions to which you aspire. Very large, flashy jewelry on any part of the body is viewed as unprofessional in many fields. Understated accessories are best.

Your perfume or cologne should also be understated. You want people to notice your accomplishments, not your perfume. Good grooming may of course include the use of scent—just be restrained. It is far more important to have clean clothes, hair, and fingernails. Make the effort. Show that you care about your appearance.

If you still question the importance of appearance in attaining a leadership position, consider this: a will-

ingness to present a leaderlike appearance demon-
strates maturity. Certainly *that* is an undeniable characteristic of a leader.

YOUR BODY LANGUAGE SAYS IT ALL

"Kelly, take this file to Mr. Eckhart's office," requested
her manager. "Be sure you deliver it to him person-
ally. He likes to meet new staffers."

When Kelly had started work the previous week,
Mr. Eckhart, head of her division, had been away on a
business trip. Now Kelly waited nervously in his
reception area. Meeting new people had always been
hard for Kelly, especially when the person was a superior. "Thank goodness I'm wearing this blazer," Kelly
thought. "At least I look like I belong here. But I sure
don't feel like I do." She slumped further down in her
seat and stared at the file she was holding.

When Mr. Eckhart came to his doorway, Kelly
pushed herself out of her low chair. As he extended
his hand, Kelly began to give him the file—until she
realized he was offering to shake hands. Embarrassed,
she looked down at her shoes and put her hand
limply in his. "It's very nice to meet you," she nearly
whispered. Then, handing him the file, she continued to stare at it as he welcomed her to the com-

pany. After he wished her a good day, she thanked him and fled the reception area. Mr. Eckhart just shook his head and returned to his office.

Kelly's body language gave a very negative impression to Mr. Eckhart. With conscious effort, you can learn to inspire confidence through positive body language. Stand and sit up straight. Act as if you deserve to be noticed. At the same time, be sure to notice others. Don't look down or away from someone—look him right in the eye. Eye contact inspires trust; lack of it makes you look suspicious. "Just shy," you say? Leaders are not shy. So practice if you must. If you pretend to be comfortable, eventually you will be. And when you are comfortable, it puts others at ease.

Always offer your hand to someone ... a handshake is ... a friendship gesture and a professional courtesy. It's an open, welcoming gesture that makes people feel more comfortable around you.
—Bradley G. Richardson,
Jobsmarts for Twentysomethings

Bradley Richardson suggests that you grasp a person's hand firmly, give a squeeze and hold until the other person breaks away or releases pressure. And of course, look the person right in the eye while you're doing it.

When we look someone in the eye, it also indicates we are paying attention to him. Maintaining that eye contact shows we are interested in what a person has to say. Leaning slightly toward a person has the same effect. Active listening is a characteristic of all good leaders.

SPEAK LIKE A LEADER

Leaders must also be able to communicate their ideas to others. Becoming an effective speaker takes effort, practice, and sometimes even professional training. But even if you do not foresee giving speeches in public, it's important to be aware of *how* you speak. People judge us on the way we talk, as well as what we say. For better or worse, our manner of speaking creates an instant impression on others.

Many speech "problems" are really just bad habits. Adding words such as "um," "like," and "you know" is common. Ask a friend to listen to you speak for one minute. Any of those useless additions? Possibly not, if you are monitoring yourself. Extend the period of time—any additions, stammering, or repetitions now?

Your goal, of course, is for *no* unnecessary words or sounds, no matter what the length of time. If you can't achieve that when only a friend is listening, imagine the difficulty you'll have when someone important is within earshot. In fact, the pressure of speaking when it "matters" is often what triggers those offending extras.

Nervous gestures, such as touching your face or hair, wringing your hands and other kinds of fidgeting, are also "extras" that should be avoided. When a confident presence is called for, nervous habits give us away.

Another annoying habit is speaking too fast. Again, this often is only a problem when under pressure. Most people talk faster when they are nervous. But if your normal conversational tempo is speedy, practice slowing down. "Speed-talk" can come across as flippant or even evasive.

Slang may also be regarded as flippant. Take care to limit slang to only those words you hear commonly used by your superiors. Foul language, on the other hand, has no place in the workplace. Never curse, even if you hear a superior curse continually.

EXERCISE

Eliminating an unwanted habit starts with recognizing that you have it. Have someone you respect give you a brutally honest appraisal of your current way of speaking. Tell him what you are trying to avoid. Ask him to point it out if you slip in the future.

LEARNING LEADERSHIP ON THE JOB

Since all leadership positions involve working with others, consider your coworkers a training ground for practicing leadership skills. Be willing to run the meeting, if it's all the same to them. But don't be too aggressive or lecture to your coworkers. Learn to listen and observe, rather than talk too much. Leaders know that the more you talk, the less others listen. Listening has the added benefit of helping you become better informed. When you do speak, you will have something intelligent to say.

LISTENING TO SUPERIORS

Listening and observing when your superiors are around has many benefits.

1. The more time you spend listening, the less likely you are to say something truly stupid or inappropriate.
2. You can learn the proper use of any "buzz-words" used commonly in your job.
3. You may learn what personal qualities your superiors admire and what skills they think most important in your field.
4. You have the opportunity to observe a superior in leadership behaviors.

ROLE MODELS

One way to learn leadership skills is by studying them in others and then modeling your behavior on theirs. A person you respect and admire can become your *role model*. The skills she exhibits in her role as leader makes her a person after whom you want to model yourself. Reverse role models also can teach us—how *not* to do something. Choosing a role model is serious business.

"I know I have a lot to learn. I'm still a baby in this business," says Lindsay. "But I'm willing to learn. Some of my peers kind of teased me for being so quiet when I first started here. But I figured if I didn't have something useful to say, I'd be better off just listening. At meetings, I noticed which people seemed to have the respect of the management. I watched how they acted—none of them were big talkers either. But when they did speak, people listened."

Lindsay adds: "In my department, one woman in particular impressed me. I began to pay attention to how she handled things, what kind of assignments she volunteered for and so on. I learned some really helpful ways of dealing with coworkers just by watching her. She recently got a well-deserved promotion to another department. I miss having her close by. Even though I'm more sure of myself now, I'm on the lookout for a new role model."

No matter how much we think we know, there is always more to learn. If you want to learn how to lead, select a role model that others respect and follow.

EXERCISE

Think about role models that you have observed in work situations. Write down how a positive model has helped you to learn ways of working more effectively.

Then think of a negative model—one who showed you how not to do something.

MENTORS

Sometimes the role models you choose are not even aware you are modeling your behavior on theirs. In other cases, a role model may offer to show you the ropes. He takes a more direct interest in your needs and offers his experience to help you in your career. He will be a wise advisor and counselor—a mentor.

A mentor knows what you need to do to reach your goals and can teach you what you need to know to get ahead in your field. Besides imparting actual know-how to help you do your job, a mentor will share his experienced view of how your company works. He will tutor you in the ways of the business world. A mentor is like a coach—he will encourage you, push you and show you ways to be more effective. And the best mentor is also a promoter. He will be your champion within the company, making sure that you have opportunities to learn and grow.

How does one find such a knight in shining armor? Sometimes a mentor will find *you*. Some companies have formalized mentoring programs. They automatically assign senior employees to mentor younger, less-experienced workers. These companies realize the value of supporting and developing those who will be the company's future leaders.

(Courtesy: Kelly Services)

When starting a career, having a role model or "mentor" will help you develop your skills, correct weaknesses and smooth the way for you in the organization. A good mentor is objective about your abilities and will advise and encourage you to reach your goals.

116

Jayne E. Hill, vice president and branch manager of the Chubb Group of Insurance Companies, is always looking for leadership potential in her employees. Featured in the article "The Boss as Mentor," in *Nation's Business* magazine, she tells author Howard Rothman that "Chubb puts a real emphasis on developing its people."

Hill takes a long-term interest in those she mentors. She gets to know their goals and needs, skills and deficiencies. She once convinced an employee to enroll in a course in communication skills. A good mentor is objective in evaluating your abilities, and will give you honest feedback about your performance.

Everyone will benefit from having a mentor, but for anyone interested in leadership in a company, a mentor is essential. So don't wait indefinitely to be "found." Be willing to take the initiative. Go about finding a mentor rationally.

Can your boss be your mentor? Ideally, every boss is a mentor to some extent. It is certainly in your boss's best interest that you perform well in your job. But mentoring also involves helping you become more visible in your company, and not every boss is in a position or has the desire to do this. The staff of

STEPS FOR FINDING A MENTOR

1. Consider your abilities objectively. What skills do you have and where do you think they will take you in your company?

2. Observe who has knowledge and influence in that area.

3. Approach a senior employee whose business style seems similar to your own. Let this individual know what your interests and goals are, and that you would welcome his advice and counsel.

4. If he seems willing to be a resource for you, you may be on your way to a mentor relationship.

Catalyst, in their book *Making the Most of Your First Job,* cites numerous successful relationships in which the boss was also the mentor. However, they caution, "Don't try to force your boss into becoming your mentor if the willingness isn't there. It may be that your boss feels uneasy singling you out as his or her protégé over your coworkers. Or perhaps your career ambitions conflict with your boss's. Whatever the reason, if you sense reluctance on the part of your boss, search for your mentor in the ranks of higher management or in another department.

MAKING AND TAKING OPPORTUNITIES

In the meantime, there are things you can do on your own to develop leadership skills. As mentioned earlier, positive interaction with your coworkers is essential. If you have a relationship of mutual trust with your peers, they will tell you their honest opinion of your endeavors—plus those of anyone else in the company! In *On Leadership,* John W. Gardner focuses on the value of coming to truly know your coworkers: "If [young people] are to be leaders, they must come to learn how other workers feel about their jobs, how they regard those above them in the hierarchy, what motivates them, what lifts their morale and what lowers it. For all of that, the workplace is a learning laboratory."

The workplace is also where you will learn the practical side of your business. Unlike school assignments, which usually ask you to practice something you have already been taught, work assignments often require you to learn something newin order to solve a problem. Since problem solving is an important ability for leadership, a mentor would steer you into these desirable assignments. If you don't have a mentor, try to get as great a variety of assignments as possible. You may even want to volunteer to take on an assignment from another department.

The organization concerned to develop its young potential leaders reassigns them periodically with a view to posing new challenges, testing new skills and introducing them to new constituencies.

—John W. Gardner, *On Leadership*

One way to build a constituency, or following, is to volunteer to lead a committee. If this opportunity does not present itself at work, you may want to seek out a community service leadership position. Just remember that no one likes a dictator. In Gardner's words, people like the leader to play a "first among equals" role.

Another way to attract followers is to become an expert at a particular task or procedure—and always be willing to help others with it. This does not mean that you become narrow in your interests and abilities. In fact, a leader needs to become a generalist—one who has knowledge of many aspects of an organization's operation.

People like the leader to play a "first among equals" role.

Make yourself a resource who people rely on and can go to for questions, information, special expertise, or access to information.

—**Bradley G. Richardson,**
Jobsmarts for Twentysomethings

TRAINING PROGRAMS

Many companies have training programs to develop leadership skills. A 1991 survey in *Training Magazine* showed that 64% of U.S. companies with 100 or more employees provided some type of training in areas related to leadership: of these companies, 69% offered training specifically in leadership skills, 61% in team building, 59% in listening skills, and 53% in problem solving.

Some companies conduct periodic appraisal interviews. These evaluations should not only assess the employee's abilities and achievements, but also provide specific recommendations for future improvement. Companies that do not specifically rate leadership abilities usually evaluate related categories such as getting along with peers and communication skills.

Ultimately, leadership is about awareness of others.

LEADERSHIP DEVELOPMENT

The development of leadership ability follows many paths, but it begins with self-awareness. You can help yourself learn to lead by viewing your talents and image objectively, and by observing and imitating the leadership qualities of role models and mentors.

But ultimately, leadership is about awareness of others—those you aspire to lead. You must be sensitive to the feelings and needs of those who are to follow. Build your team based on mutual trust and respect. Offer positive feedback as well as constructive criticism; be willing to learn from subordinates as well as superiors. A leader cannot truly succeed without the support of those he leads.

GLOSSARY

Active listening. Ways during a conversation, such as eye contact and leaning toward a speaker, that imply interest and attention.

Brainstorming. A problem-solving technique in which various members of a group offer up spontaneous ideas.

Constituency. A following or group of supporters.

Constructively competitive. Being competitive without alienating others; competition that is helpful toward achieving the final goal.

Feedback. Opinions of others on a person's performance.

Flow chart. An organizational tool that shows a step-by-step progression to solve a problem or procedure.

Gantt chart. Chart showing the timing of both simultaneous and sequential tasks and the relative amount of time allotted for each.

Mentor. A wise adviser and counselor who serves as a role model in a personal or business setting.

Multitask. Consisting of many tasks.

Notebook tracking. Using a notebook to track the progress of a project or task.

Purchase order (P. O.). A document or form required for the buying of goods or services.

Role model. A person whose behavior is observed and imitated.

Tasks-by-levels chart. An organizational tool that divides tasks by levels and puts them into columns.

BIBLIOGRAPHY

Bliss, Edwin C. *Getting Things Done: The ABC's of Time Management.* New York: Bantam Books, 1995.

Day, Carol, ed. and the staff of Catalyst. *Making the Most of Your First Job.* New York: G. P. Putnam's Sons, 1981.

Ellis, Darryl J. and Peter P. Pekar, Jr.. *Planning for Nonplanners.* New York: AMACOM, 1980.

Fournies, Ferdinand. *Why Employees Don't Do What They're Supposed to Do and What to Do About It.* Blue Ridge Summit, PA: Liberty House, 1988.

Gardner, John W. *On Leadership.* New York: The Free Press, 1990.

Hogan, Robert, Joyce Hogan, and Gordon J. Curphy. "What We Know About Leadership," *American Psychologist,* June 1994, pp. 493–504.

Killian, Ray A. "The Practice of Leadership," in *Leadership on the Job,* William K. Fallon, ed. New York: AMACOM, 1981.

Levering, Robert and Milton Moskowitz. *The 100 Best Companies to Work for in America.* New York: Doubleday, 1993.

Manz, Charles C. and Henry Sims. *SuperLeadership: Leading Others to Lead Themselves.* New York: Prentice Hall, 1989.

McLean, J. W. *Leadership: Magic, Myth, or Method.* New York: AMACOM, 1991.

Richardson, Bradley G. *Jobsmarts for Twentysomethings.* New York: Random House, 1995.

Rothman, Howard. "The Boss as Mentor," *Nation's Business,* April 1993, pp.66–67.

Syrett, Michael and Clare Hogg. *Frontiers of Leadership.* Cambridge, Mass.: Blackwell, 1992.

Wagner, Richard K. and Robert J. Sternberg, *Measures of Leadership.* New York: Leadership Library of America, Inc., 1991.

Welsh, Alexander N. *The Skills of Management.* New York: AMACOM, 1981.

Winston, Stephanie. *The Organized Executive.* New York: Warner Books, 1994.